1 795060 2

D1102974

RENFREWSHIRE COUNCIL	
179506021	
Bertrams	27/06/2011
	£7.99
FER	

NOT BAD FOR A
BAD LAD

To Jo Dixon for getting me in,
the prisoners and staff of Hollesley Bay for letting me out again,
and Keith Tarrant for 'inside' information! – M.F.

To Kay, Hanan, Nima, Yasin and Nadia – M.M.

A TEMPLAR BOOK

First published in the UK in 2010 by Templar Publishing
This softback edition published in 2010 by Templar Publishing,
an imprint of The Templar Company Limited,
The Granary, North Street, Dorking, Surrey, RH4 1DN, UK
www.templarco.co.uk

Illustration copyright © 2010 by Michael Foreman
Text copyright © 2010 by Michael Morpurgo

3 5 7 9 10 8 6 4 2

All rights reserved

ISBN 978-1-84877-312-7

Drum major's insignia artwork by Chris Forsey
Designed by Mike Jolley
Edited by Anne Finnis
Consultant Chris Miller

Printed in China

Michael Morpurgo

NOT BAD FOR A
BAD LAD

Illustrated by **Michael Foreman**

templar publishing

THIS IS THE STORY OF MY LIFE. I've written it
so you'll know all the things about your grandpa that
you've got a right to know and that I never told you.
There's no two ways about it: when I was young I
was a bad lad. I'm not proud of it, not one bit.
Grandma has been saying for quite a while now that
it's about time I told you everything, the truth, the
whole truth and nothing but the truth – before it's too
late, she says. So here goes.

I was born in 1943, on the 5th of October. But
you don't want to know that. It was a long time ago,
that's all, when the world was a very different place.
A whole lifetime ago for me.

I had a dad, of course I did, but I never met him.
He just wasn't there, so I didn't miss him. Well maybe
I did, maybe I just didn't know it at the time. Ma had
six children. I was number four and I was always a
bad lad, right from the start. Down our street there
was this bomb site – there were lots of houses around
us all bombed to bits in the war. There was a sign up

outside the bomb site. It said: 'Danger. Keep Out'.
Well of course I went in, didn't I? And that's because
it was the best place to play. I'm telling you, it was
supreme. I could climb the walls, I could make dens,
I could chase butterflies, and when Ma called me in
for my tea I could hide away and pretend I wasn't
there. I remember the local copper. He was called PC
Nightingale – some names you don't forget – and he
would come in after me sometimes and chase me out.
He'd shout it out all down the street how he'd give me
a right good hiding if he ever caught me in there again.

When I was old enough to go to school, to St
Matthias, down the road, I discovered pretty quick
that I didn't like it, or they didn't like me – a bit of
both, I reckon. That's why I bunked off school
whenever I could, whenever I felt like it, which was
quite often. The School Attendance Officer would
come round to the house and complain to Ma about
me. Sometimes he'd threaten to take me away and
put me in a home, then Ma would get all upset and yell
at me, and I'd yell back at her. We did a lot of yelling,

Ma and me. I'd tell her how the teachers were
always having a go at me, whatever I was
doing, whenever I opened my mouth, that they
whacked me with a ruler if I talked back, or
cheeked them, that I spent most of my lessons
standing with my face in the corner, so what
was the point of being at school anyway?

The trouble was, and I can see now
what I couldn't see then, that I turned
out to be no good at anything the
teachers wanted me to be good at.
And when I was no good they told
me I was no good, and that just
made the whole thing worse.
I couldn't do my reading.
I couldn't do my writing.
I couldn't do my arithmetic
– sums and things like
that. I was, "a brainless,
useless, good-for-nothing
waste of space".

That's what Mr Mortimer called me one day in front of the whole school and he was the head teacher, so he had to be right, didn't he?

There was only one thing I did like at school and that was the music lessons, because we had Miss West to teach us and Miss West liked me, I could tell. She was kind to me, made me feel special. She smelled of lavender and face powder and I loved that. She made me Drum Cupboard Monitor, and that meant that whenever she wanted anything from the drum cupboard, she'd give me the key and send me off to fetch a triangle, or the cymbals maybe, or the tambourines, or a drum. And what's more, she'd let me play on them too. So when all the others were tootling away on their recorders, I got to have a go on the drums, or the cymbals, or the tambourine, or the triangle – but the triangle was a bit tinkly, didn't make a loud enough noise, not for me anyway. I liked the drum best. I liked banging out the rhythm, loud, and Miss West told me I had a really good sense of rhythm, that drums and me were made for one another, even if I was sometimes, she said, "a wee bit over-enthusiastic".

Then Miss West left the school – I don't know why – and that made me very sad. I still played the drums whenever I could, and I was still Drum Cupboard Monitor, but none of it was nearly so much fun without Miss West. I never forgot her though, and you'll see why soon enough.

I was that keen on drumming by now that I began to find ways of doing it out of school. At home I'd play the spoons all the time, and drive Ma half barmy with it. When she sent me out, I'd do it with sticks on the railings, or on dustbin lids. Dustbin lids were best because if I banged them hard enough I could make a din like thunder that echoed all down the street, and sent the pigeons scattering. Some people, like Mrs Dickson who kept the shop on the corner, had two dustbins outside, so I could stand there and bang away on two dustbin lids at the same time, then I could pick them up and crash them together like cymbals. You should have heard the racket that made! But Mrs Dickson was a bit of a spoilsport. She'd come running out of her shop and tick me off. She'd shoo me away with her broom, and call me "a bad, bad lad" – and other things too that I'd better not mention.

Then I went and did something really stupid.

I stole an orange from a barrow in the market.
And what did I do? I only ran round the corner,
smack into PC Nightingale, who also told me I was
a bad lad. He took me back home, tweaking my
ear all the way, and told Ma what I had done,
and that I needed a right good walloping. So
she said I was a bad lad too and smacked me
on the back of my knees. The day after that,
things only went from bad to worse.

In school the next morning, at assembly,
Mr Mortimer told us he'd got a very
serious announcement to make, very
serious indeed. He said that PC Nightingale
had been in to see him with some very bad news,
about an orange. I knew I was in for it now. He held
up the orange I'd nicked, or one just like it, and told
everyone that they had an orange thief in the school.
I knew what was coming. He called out my name and
pointed right at me with his yellow nicotiney finger.
Everyone turned round to look at me, which I didn't
much mind – actually, to be honest, I quite enjoyed

that part of it – you know, the fame part, the recognition. After all, I was the school's chief troublemaker. That was what I was good at, being a troublemaker. I was proud of it too. I had my reputation. I was someone to be reckoned with and I liked that.

Mr Mortimer got me up there in front of everyone, and told me to hold out my hand, and then he whacked me with the ruler – which I did mind, because this time it was with the edge of the ruler, on the back of my hand, on my knuckles, and it hurt like billy-o. And, yes, you've guessed it, he told me I was a bad lad, and how I'd bought shame on myself and on the whole school. Worst of all though, he said I wasn't Drum Cupboard Monitor any more, and that I wasn't going to be allowed to play on the drums any more, nor on the cymbals, nor even on the silly triangle, not ever. Well, that was it, the final straw, that and my bruised knuckles. Now I was mad, really mad – and I'm not excusing myself – but that was why I went and did something that was even more stupid than nicking the orange in the first place.

Because I'd been Drum Cupboard Monitor, I
knew exactly where the drum cupboard key was kept,
didn't I? On the hook in the back of the teacher's
desk. So at break time I took the key, opened the
drum cupboard and pinched the biggest drum of the
lot, my favourite. Then, banging it as loud as I could,
and with the whole school watching, I marched
through the playground, out of the school gates and
down the road. I went on banging that drum all the
way home. I got expelled for that, which was all right
by me, because without Miss West there I hated the
place anyway.

The other schools Ma sent me to after that
weren't much better. The trouble was, they all
knew I was a bad lad before I even got there.
It's obvious, isn't it? They expected me to be
a troublemaker and so that's just what I was,
every time. In the end I ran out of schools that
would have me. I couldn't even begin to count
the number of times they caned me. It hurt, of
course it did. But it was water off a duck's back

to me. By the time I was fourteen I'd left school behind me and found myself a part-time job in a garage, which was all right with me because I liked cars. But at nights I was out on the streets and getting myself into all sorts of trouble and strife.

By now I'd got in with a gang of bigger kids and I wasn't nicking just oranges any more. Anything they could do, I could do better. I had to prove myself, that's how I saw it. One evening we saw this car parked in the street, a nice shiny-looking MG it was. It wasn't locked and the driver had left his key in the ignition. Well, I was used to cars, wasn't I? I knew a little bit about them. So, just to show off to the other kids, I got in and drove it away. Simple. I roared around the place for half an hour or so, until I hit the kerb and got a puncture. I was just about to get out and leg it, when I saw this pen lying there on the passenger seat – gold topped it was with a gold arrow, very smart, and must be worth a bit too, I thought. So I pocketed it and then got out of there, smartish. Before I went home I

flogged the pen outside The Horse and Plough, the pub
down our street, and for the very first time in my life,
I had proper money in my hand. Five shillings I got
for it. All right, that's only twenty-five pence in today's
money, but that was a lot then, a small fortune to me.

Next thing I knew, the police came round to our
house that evening to question me. They said someone
had seen me that afternoon getting out of a stolen
car. I told them I'd been at home all the time, and
that anyway, I didn't know how to drive. They went
and searched the house, but they didn't find anything.
I'd hidden my five shillings in the water cistern above
the lavvy out the back – y'know, the toilet. They were
always out the back in those days.

When they'd gone Ma gave me the rollicking of my
life. She took me by the shoulders and shook me till
my teeth rattled. She said she knew I'd done it.
"You weren't home this afternoon, were you? You
lied, didn't you? I should have told them, I should
have." She was crying and shouting at the same time,

really angry with me she was. "Reform school, Borstal, that's where you belong. Maybe they can knock some sense into you, because I can't. You're nothing but trouble. You can't be good like other kids, can you? Oh no, you've got to go nicking stuff, thieving, lying. Where d'you think that's going to get you anyway? Crime doesn't pay. Never did. Don't you know that? Don't you know anything?"

Ma was so upset I was worried she might go after the coppers and tell them. But she didn't, thank goodness. So I was in the clear. I'd got away with it. After that, I got away with it again and again. Most of the others in our gang were a lot older than me, and a whole lot better at thieving than I was. But I was learning fast, all the tricks of the burgling trade: how you choose your house, take your time in staking it out, prise open windows, pick door locks and break into safes. And you had to know who the fences were because you had to get rid of the loot, all the stolen stuff, the incriminating stuff as quick as possible. In only a year or two I was a fully trained thief and a bad lad

through and through. But there was one thing I never learned properly: how not to get caught.

For maybe a year or so, everything looked as if it was working out fine. I was doing very nicely thank you. Who says crime doesn't pay, Ma? That's what I was thinking. I had more than enough money to buy anything and everything I wanted: flash suits, flash watch and flash motorbike. I could show-off to everyone at home, brag about how well I was doing to anyone who would listen. The girls were taking quite a fancy to me too, and I didn't mind that either, not one bit. They all thought I was quite a lad. I even bought Ma one of those new-fangled television sets. She was mighty pleased with that, I can tell you. Quite proud of me she was, but that was only because she thought I'd gone back to my old job at the garage, because that's what I'd told her. She never knew where the money came from, nor what I was getting up to. Mind you, she never asked. Thinking back now, I reckon that might have been because she didn't *want* to know. She wasn't stupid, my Ma.

Then one night my luck ran out. I'd done a good
clean job, in and out of an empty house, quiet as a
mouse, no one there, no bother. I'd nicked some silver
and some jewellery, nice stuff too. Everything seemed
tickety-boo. But as I was coming away from the house
I saw this copper riding towards me on his bike. I
should have just walked on by – he wouldn't have
even noticed I was there. But oh no, I had to go and
make a run for it. First rule in the book: always
walk away from a job, never run. He blew his
whistle and I was off down the road, going
like a greyhound. He chased after me, over
a building site, across a railway line. I
chucked away all the stuff I'd pinched. Lose
the evidence, that's what I was thinking,
but I couldn't lose him. In the end,
I scrambled over the wall into
someone's back garden, and
then I saw this greenhouse. So
I dived in there, nifty as you
like, and hid myself in
amongst a whole forest of

tomato plants. For a while there was a lot of shouting and dancing torchlights out there, but then it all went quiet. It was just me and a big round moon up there and tomatoes all around me. I thought I'd just lie low for a bit, until things calmed down, until I was quite sure I was in the clear.

Half an hour or so later I was still sitting there in the greenhouse, happily scoffing down a nice ripe tomato, when I looked up and saw this little boy standing there in his striped pyjamas.

"That's one of my dad's tomatoes," he said. "That's stealing, that is. You're the one the coppers were after, aren't you? You're a bad'n, I know you are."

And then, before I could stop him, he ran for it, shouting his head off. In no time at all there were coppers everywhere and they took me away. I got sentenced to a year in Borstal for breaking and entering. It would have been more if Miss West hadn't come and spoken up for me.

It was very kind of her, but I felt so ashamed of myself when I saw her coming into the court. I couldn't bring myself to look at her properly.

The magistrate told me just what he thought of me. "You've been a bad lad, haven't you?" he said. "However, your old teacher, Miss West, tells us you're not a bad lad at heart and I'm inclined to believe her, to give you the benefit of the doubt. But you have been stupid, that's for sure, and you've got yourself in with the wrong sort." He leaned forward and looked at me over his glasses. "You've wasted your life up until now, young man," he went on. "You're only sixteen, still young. You can make a fresh start. You can put things right if you want to. It's up to you. You'll have a year in Borstal to think things over, to learn your lesson. Take him away."

Silly old goat, I was thinking. But I knew in my heart of hearts, even as I was thinking it, that I was the silly one, not him.

So after a few nights in a police cell, they drove me away to this Borstal place, a sort of reform school I was told, somewhere in Suffolk. But I didn't much care where it was. I'd never felt more miserable in all my life. Only one thing bucked me up on that horrible journey. It was something Miss West had said about me in the court: "He's like all of us. He just needs to feel good about himself. He's got good in him, I know he has. He needs a second chance. All I'm asking is that you give him that chance. He'll come right one day, you'll see."

I kept her words in my head the whole way. Truth be told, I've kept them in my head my whole life.

There were a dozen or more of us in that Black Maria van, all lads about my age, all bad lads. None of us spoke a word the whole way. Half an hour after we arrived, they took us into the gym and told us to change into the blue uniforms they'd given us. Then in he came.

"My name's Sir," he barked. We found out later that he did have a proper name, Mr Roley. He looked a bit like Mr Mortimer, small with a neat little moustache under his nose, a bit like Hitler's I thought, except it was ginger. He had a voice like a trombone. We huddled together like a flock of sheep, all of us afraid. He looked at us and shook his head in disgust. "Every one of you is a bad apple. Rotten apples, the lot of you," he went on. "That's why you're here. And I'm here to cut out the bad bit, the rotten bit. Simple as that. You do as you're told. You work hard and you behave yourselves, and you've got nothing to

worry about. You can be happy as you like in here.
But you give me any trouble, any lip, any attitude,
then I'll make you wish you'd never been born. Is
that quite clear? And just to be sure I make
myself clear, I'm going to do you a favour.
I'm going to show you what'll happen to
any of you if you step out of line."
Suddenly, he was pointing right at
me. "You, in the front. Over
here! Now!"

Ten of the best
with a cane he gave
me, stretched over
the wooden
vaulting horse.
Worst beating
I ever had.
It hurt like
hell, but
I never
let on.

I didn't want to give him the satisfaction. It went on hurting for days afterwards. But when all's said and done, I reckon it was all my fault in the first place. I shouldn't have been at the front, should I?

I can tell you that during those first weeks locked up in Borstal I did an awful lot of hard thinking. My head was full of questions that I couldn't answer. How did I get to be here? Was this how I was going to spend the rest of my life from now on, behind the walls of a prison, shut off from the rest of the world? Which was I, stupid or bad, or both? Or was Miss West right? Did I have some good in me?

I don't think I spoke a word to anyone in that place for a month or more. I felt like I was sleepwalking through it all, the two-mile run every morning, laying bricks for hours on end in all weathers, making bread in the kitchens, weeding in the vegetable garden, Mr Roley and the others watching us like hawks the whole time. They never let up on us. We didn't have a moment to ourselves. But the worst thing wasn't the

work, nor Mr Roley, nor the food, which was always about as disgusting as they could make it, I reckon. It was listening to one of the other lads crying himself to sleep at night. That would always get me going, and I'd be crying myself then. I just couldn't help it.

There were twenty other lads in my dormitory. I didn't want to speak to any of them in the early days. I didn't want to know them. Some nights I turned my face to the wall and just wished I was dead. And when I wasn't wishing I was dead, I was dreaming of bunking off, doing a runner, like I sometimes used to do at St Matthias when I got into trouble. But I knew there was no point. I mean, where would I go? Ma didn't want me at home any more, I knew that. And besides, one or two of the other lads had already tried it, and they were always brought back. True to his word, Mr Roley would have them in the gym and give them ten of the best and we'd have to stand there and watch it too.

So after a while I stopped thinking about running off and I decided I would make the best of a bad job: just do my time, keep my head down, and keep myself out of trouble. My favourite part of every day was the two-mile run we had to do before breakfast, because that's when we got to go outside the walls, and even down to the beach sometimes, which was only a mile or so away. I liked running, and running fast too, running like I'd never stop. I liked the beach too, and the sea air, and the gulls, and the fishing boats out at sea. All the while I could make-believe I was free, free as the gulls. The other lads – and most of them really hated that early morning run – told me I must be mad to like it, bonkers, off my rocker, but they could say what they liked, I didn't mind.

There was one place on the run where I sometimes used to slow down to get a better look: the stables. It was a funny thing (and when I think about it, which I do a lot, it was a pretty wonderful thing really), but this Borstal place had some stables, horses' stables, where a few of the lads used to come to work for a few hours each day. Every time I ran past there, the horses would be looking out at me, with their heads over the stable doors, and their ears pricked. It was like they were waiting for me to run by. They would look at me and I would look at them. They'd have a good old whinny at me sometimes too and I'd wave back – pretty silly I know, but I could hardly whinny, could I? There was a bit of a whiff coming out of those stables, I can tell you. But I quite liked the smell of horses, always did. It reminded me of the milkman's horse in our street. Lovely fellow he was – the horse not the milkman.

From time to time, as I ran by, I'd see this old bloke in there with the horses. I knew he was old because he had silvery hair and a moustache to match. Very smart and tidy he always was, the sort of fellow who looked after himself. Everyone called him Mr Alfie, but that's all I knew about him. I'd seen a few of the lads working in there with him and I'd often thought that wouldn't be a bad old job if I could get it, better than bricklaying or baking anyway.

But there was something else that really interested me every time I ran past those stables. There was always music. Mr Alfie would be out there in the yard, pushing a wheelbarrow, or grooming the horses, or shovelling muck, and there'd often be music playing on the radio – 'wireless' they called it in those days. It was big bands mostly, or jazz, and it was the kind of music I liked, lots of rhythm, and lots of drumming too. And when Mr Alfie had the music on I wouldn't be running by at all, I'd be trotting, then walking, slowly, very slowly, so I could listen for as long as possible.

One day – and as it turned out it was just about the luckiest day of my life – I was out on the morning run as usual and coming past the stables when I heard the music playing again. I'd slowed right down to a walk and that's when I saw this Mr Alfie bloke standing there by the fence watching me, mopping his brow with his handkerchief. He called me over, so I went.

"You like horses, son?" he asked me.

"They're all right." I told him. "Bit smelly."

"Of course they are, son. But do you like them?"

"I suppose so."

"You want to give us a hand with them then?"

"What now?"

"Tomorrow," Mr Alfie said. "You can start tomorrow. I need another pair of hands. I'll speak to Mr Roley. I've been watching you out on your run and I thought you liked horses. Every time you come past here, you always slow down and have a good long look."

"That's because of the music, on the wireless," I told him. "I like music. I like drumming. I play the drums – I used to anyway."

"Well, there's a thing. I'm a bit of a drummer myself," Mr Alfie said. "Tell you the truth, there's only one thing I like more than my music, and that's my horses. Suffolk Punch horses they are and they take a lot of looking after. You don't mind hard work do you?"

"'Course not," I told him.

So that's how, the very next day after breakfast, I
found myself helping out in the stables, along with a
couple of other lads, giving Mr Alfie a hand with his
horses. He'd fixed it up with Mr Roley, just as he'd said
he would. From now on, for most of every day, I'd be
working with those great big beautiful horses, alongside
Mr Alfie. I loved it, loved the horses, loved listening to
the music, loved every moment of it all. Mind you,
having to leave the horses and go back behind the
walls afterwards was always hard, really hard.

I think maybe I should tell you something about
Mr Alfie and his horses, because without them none
of the rest of this story would have turned out the
way it did. I soon found out that Mr Alfie knew more
about Suffolk horses than any man alive. He'd even
written a book about them. He knew them and he
loved them. And these Suffolk horses aren't your
ordinary horses. They are gigantic, I mean massive.
They stand higher than your head, however tall you
are. And they're strong. You cannot believe how
strong they are. Mr Alfie had grown up with them on

the farm when he was a kid and he'd worked with horses of one kind or another, practically all his life, ploughing the fields, mowing the hay. He'd left the farm for a while, to go and fight in the First World War. He'd been there with horses too, mostly with cavalry horses he told me. But for Mr Alfie, his Suffolk horses were always the best. "My gentle giants," he used to call them.

Every time we went down to the stables we'd be mucking them out, shaking out the straw for their bedding, putting up the hay for them or filling their water buckets. And did they eat a lot, those horses! Did they drink a lot! And did they make a mess! I'd never been kept so busy in all my life and I'd never enjoyed myself so much either, specially when Mr Alfie had his music on. But he kept us at it. We'd be cleaning the tack, polishing the brasses, doing whatever needed doing, and there was always something.

After a while, a couple of weeks it must have been, Mr Alfie began to let me do some of the grooming, and soon enough I was out with the other lads, who'd been stable lads longer than me, exercising the horses, even riding them out sometimes. All the time, he was teaching us how to behave around horses. "You have to treat them the same way you have to treat people," he told me once. "First you have to try to understand what's going on in their heads, what they're feeling. Then you have to respect those feelings. Do that with anyone, and you'll get on fine. Do it with any horse

and you'll get on fine. It's as simple as that." Of
course it wasn't at all simple, because what he didn't
tell me was that it takes a lifetime to get to know how
horses feel. I know now that it takes a lifetime to get
to know how people feel too. So Mr Alfie was right,
twice over.

I reckon I must have been working with the horses
for a couple of months or so, and was getting the
hang of things quite well. I arrived at the stables one
morning and got to work right away, grooming Bella

out in the yard – she was the biggest of the mares we had in the stables: eighteen hands high, and that's big, too big to argue with that's for sure. Anyway I looked up and there was Mr Alfie coming towards me. He stood and watched me for a while, not saying anything. He did that quite a bit, so I wasn't bothered. The wireless was playing as usual, a Louis Armstrong number: 'Jeepers Creepers'.

I remember that very well because the next moment what Mr Alfie said to me next has stayed in my mind ever since. "You know what I think son?" he said. "I think you're not bad for a bad lad, not a bad lad at all." Those few words meant more to me then than I can ever say. They still do. "When you've finished with Bella," he went on, "I've got a bit of a job for you." A few minutes later he was walking me to the end stable.

"In here," he said, opening the door. "He came in last night. Five-year-old, he is. Dombey, he's called. He's not a Suffolk, but he's as good as. Not quite as big maybe, but the same type. Brown and white.

'Skewbald', we call that. Handsome looking fellow isn't he? But he's a bit upset." I could see that. Unlike all the other horses, who were always looking out over their stable doors, all bright-eyed and happy, this one was standing with his head down, in the darkest corner of the stable.

"Where he's come from they couldn't manage him," Mr Alfie told me. "He's a bit of a handful it seems. Dombey's had a hard time. Someone's taken a stick to him, that's what I think. But he's strong as you like, kind eye, big heart. He's a good sort. I know a good sort when I see one. That's why I've taken him on. That's why I took you on. But Dombey's frit, and he's miserable. He's off his food too. All he needs is someone he can trust, someone who can understand him and gentle him. So I thought, why not you? I want you just to spend time with him, son, talk to him, give him a pat, tell him he's a good lad, make him feel he's wanted. He's got to feel

like someone loves him. But watch him, mind. They say he's got a mighty powerful kick on him."

Only the next morning I was to find that out for myself. I thought I was doing everything just right. I went into the stable nice and slow, talking to him all the while. His tail swished a bit, so I knew he was a bit nervy. I stood by his head for a long time, just whispering to him, smoothing his neck, stroking his ears gently. He liked that, everything was fine. He looked

happy enough to have me there. After a bit I thought
that was probably enough for a first meeting. I was
feeling quite pleased with myself. I gave him a goodbye
pat and walked out slowly the way I'd come in, behind
him. Big mistake. I didn't even see him kick me, but I
felt it all right. The next thing I knew I was lying there
on my back in the straw, feeling like a right nitwit.

Mr Alfie was leaning over the
stable door. "He kicked you
then?" he said, smiling down at
me. "Did it hurt?"

"What d'you think?" I told
him, rubbing at my leg to
ease away the pain.

"Well son, whatever you did, you won't do it again then, will you?" Mr Alfie said. "It'll take time. It always takes time to learn to trust someone." He wasn't showing me much sympathy. "Anyway," he went on, looking up at Dombey, who was chomping away at his hay, "Dombey seems to be eating well enough now. So he's happy about something. You must have done something right then." That was the thing about Mr Alfie, he always said something to buck you up and make you feel better about yourself.

It took time, just like Mr Alfie had said, for Dombey and me to learn to get along, months of talking to him, of grooming him, of exercising him, of just being with him. He never kicked me again, but then I never gave him cause. I never walked behind him again in the stable. I got to know his little ways, and he got to know mine. He grew to be as bold and as bright-eyed as the others, always looking out over the stable door whenever I came into the yard, waiting for me.

I made two good friends in that stable yard, two of
the best I ever had.

Dombey and me became like brothers. I was never so happy in all my life than when I was riding Dombey along the beach. Mr Alfie gave me special permission to do that. He told me I should gallop him through the shallows. He needed it, he said. It would be good for him to stretch his legs and build up his strength. Dombey loved every moment of it and so did I. In one way, he was like a little brother to me, because I was looking after him. But then in another way he was my big brother, because he was big. When he pushed me or shoved me or nudged me, it was only gently and only ever in fun, just to let me know from time to time that this little brother was also a big brother too, and I'd better remember it. I always did.

As for Mr Alfie, well he became the father I never had. And I wasn't treated any different than the others. He was like that with all of us, all the lads who worked in his yard. Just so long as we worked hard, just so long as we did all we could for his 'gentle giants', then he treated us like we were family, like proper family, and most of us had never had that.

Then one morning when I was mucking out
Bella's stable, Mr Alfie came over to me and said he
wanted a word. He put his arm round my shoulder as
we walked away, so I knew something was up, that
something was wrong.

"I've got a bit of sad news, son, and a bit of glad
news as well," he said. "Sad news first, eh? Best to get
it over with quick. Dombey's been sold, son. They're
coming to take him away in a couple of hours. But
the glad news is that if things turn out as I think they
will, then he'll have a good home for life and a job for
life – I'd say just about the best job and the best home
a horse could have. And that'll be down to you, son.
You've made him a happy horse. The rest was inside
him already, all his strength, all his kindness, in his
blood you might say. But you made him happy, so he
behaves himself now, and where he's going that'll be
very important."

"Where is he going?" I asked.
"I can't tell you that, son, not yet," Mr Alfie said.

"It's all very hush-hush for the moment. They've been to see him and they think he's just right, just the horse they're looking for. They're taking him on trial for six months, but if he's the horse I think he is and he behaves himself, then they'll keep him. That's all I can tell you at the moment. Don't you go worrying yourself about Dombey, son. There won't be a horse in the land better looked after and that's a promise."

I don't mind telling you that once Mr Alfie had
gone I went into Dombey's stable, sat down in the
straw and sobbed my heart out. Dombey came over
to me and nuzzled at my neck to try to cheer me up.
Everyone in the yard, all the other lads, knew how I
felt about Dombey. They'd ribbed me about him
often enough, how we spent so much time together
that the two of us were practically married. But they
weren't teasing me any more now. They all had their
favourites and they knew well enough how bad I must
be feeling.

Later that morning in the stable, I gave Dombey one last hug and told him he was going somewhere where he would be happy, but that he was on trial, so he'd got to behave himself. Mr Alfie let me lead him up into the lorry, where I said my last goodbyes. As they drove him out of the yard we heard him give the tailboard of the lorry a thumping great kick. We all of us laughed at that, which was just as well, because I'd have cried again otherwise.

"You will let me know how he gets on, won't you?" I asked Mr Alfie as I left the stable that afternoon.

"Of course I will, son," he said.

But he never did, because when I got to the yard the next day, they told me that Mr Alfie was off sick and he wouldn't be back for a while. I never got to see him again. A few days later I had a nice surprise. Mr Roley called me in. They'd decided to let me out early, three months early, for good behaviour. Of course I was pleased as punch about that, over the moon, but I never got to say goodbye to Mr Alfie.

Something very strange happens, I
discovered, when you come out after you've
been locked up. Everyone looks at you, in the
street, on the buses, in the shops, as if they
know where you've been. But do you know
what's worse still? You don't feel like you
belong anywhere. You feel like a stray dog.
They gave me a room in a hostel – poky little
place, more like a kennel it was. I didn't know
where to go, nor what to do with myself. I couldn't go
home, because they didn't want to see me any more –
I can't blame them, not really.

For a couple of months I just wandered the streets
getting to know all the other stray people – and
there's lots of them out there, believe you me – who
were doing much the same thing as me, wandering
the streets and wishing the days away. Some of them
had been on the streets for years. I didn't want to end
up like them, but I knew that's the way I was heading
and I didn't think there was much I could do about it.

Then one warm summer evening, I decided it
might be an idea to go into the park and find myself
a nice park bench where I could spend the night. I
was fed up with the four walls of my stuffy little room
at the hostel. I lay there that night looking up at
the stars and I remember thinking about
Mr Alfie, and hoping he was better, and
about Dombey, wondering where he'd
gone, whether he was behaving himself
and who was looking after him now. And
I was wondering too where Miss West was
these days, and whether I'd ever
see anything of any of them ever
again. I went to sleep. The first
thing I heard when I woke up
was the sound of trotting
horses, lots of snorting and
snuffling, and jingling
harnesses, and a whinny or two
as well. I sat up. I thought I must
still be dreaming. But I wasn't.

There were dozens of horses coming towards me
in twos, one of each pair being ridden, the other
being led. As they came closer I could see there were
soldiers riding them, all in khaki uniforms, with
peaked caps. They trotted right past me. The horses
were magnificent, not big sturdy Suffolk horses like
Mr Alfie's, but sleek-looking thoroughbreds with
shining coats and tossing heads. None of the soldiers
spoke to me as they rode by, except for the last
one, who wasn't leading a second horse like all
the others – and that was just as well, I was
thinking, because the horse he was riding was
really playing up. All wild-eyed and skippy and
up on his toes he was.

"Nice morning," said the soldier. And that's all
he had time to say, because that's when it
happened, just as he was talking to me.

Suddenly this dog came charging out
of the trees from behind my
bench, barking his head off,

a little scruffy-looking thing he was. Well of course
that skippy horse took one look at him, shied, reared
up, then threw his rider and took off into the park.

I did the first thing that came into my
head. I went after the
horse. I caught up with
him in the end, just
before he reached the
road. I was a bit puffed out
by this time. He was still quite
upset, but I could see that he had
calmed down a little, enough to be
nuzzling at the grass. I sweet-talked
him as I came towards him, just like
I'd learned to do with Dombey.

When I got close enough, I managed to smoothe his neck and stroke his ears and finally I got hold of his reins and began to walk him back. The whole column of horses had stopped by now and I saw the soldier who'd been thrown limping towards me.

"You all right?" I asked him.

"Bit knocked about, but I'll be fine. Stupid ruddy

dog," he said. "But you did well to catch my horse before he got on the road. I owe you one. He was a bit full of himself this morning. He gets like that." He took the reins from me. "You know horses, don't you?" he went on. "I mean you're really good with them. We could do with a fellow like you in the regiment. Ever fancied being a soldier?"

"What, with horses?"

"Why not?" said the soldier. "It's what I am. I get three square meals a day, and a warm bed to sleep in. Pay's not brilliant, but it'll do. We have a pretty good time, us and the horses. You should try it."

And I remembered then that Mr Alfie had been a soldier once, and with horses too.

"Maybe I will," I told him.

"Tell you what you do then," he said. "Just go down the road to that big building there beyond the trees. It's where we're headed now. Follow where the horse poos lead. You can't miss it. Ask for the duty officer. I'll tell him what's happened, tell him to expect you."

Well, I'd got nothing much else to do, had I? Why not give it a go, I thought. So that same morning I did what the soldier had said, followed the horse poos, and went along there. To cut a long story short, that's how I joined the army.

A few weeks of being shouted at and marching up and down and polishing boots and badges, a few more weeks of driving around in armoured cars, and then they let me have a go on the horses.

I could not believe my luck. From sleeping rough on a park bench to sitting up there on my shiny black horse, with a shiny helmet on my head, and a shiny breastplate to match, in a pair of the longest, shiniest, blackest boots you ever saw, and a shining sword over my shoulder. I just didn't think life could get any shinier.

But it did.

It was the day of my first big
parade, the Queen's Birthday
Parade it was, and the band was
there too. I heard them
before I saw them, the big
drum thumping away.
Then they came round

the corner, the full regimental mounted band, all of them playing their instruments, on horseback. What a sound it was! What a sight it was! And out in front of the band was this huge drum horse, a silver kettledrum on either side of him, and the Drum Major banging away on them, like he was having the time of his life. Then I looked again. I can tell you, I nearly fell off *my* horse. That drum horse was brown and white! That drum horse was a skewbald! It was Dombey! No mistake, it was my Dombey!

I sat there on my horse during that whole parade, making up my mind there and then that one day I'd be up there riding Dombey, that one day it would be me banging away on those shiny silver kettledrums.

When the parade was over I went to see Dombey in his stable. He knew me right away and I can't tell you how happy that made me.

71

It took me a few years of course, and I had to
work hard, but I got there in the end. It was the
proudest day of my life that first time riding out as
Drum Major on old Dombey – and he was
quite old by then – banging out the rhythm
for the band, the whole of London echoing
with it. As I rode along the Mall up to the
Palace, there were crowds everywhere,
clapping and smiling. They weren't
looking at me, they were looking at
Dombey – I know that.

I kept thinking all the while of Mr Alfie and Miss West, and all they'd done for me, how they'd kept faith with me, and I just hoped they were somewhere in the crowd out there and watching me. More than anything I wanted them to be proud of me. I swear I kept hearing Mr Alfie's voice in my head, saying the same thing over and over, the beat of the drum in every word:

"NOT BAD FOR A BAD LAD,
NOT A BAD LAD AT ALL."

SO NOW YOU KNOW MY WHOLE LIFE
STORY – well, most of it anyway. Of course I had
my ups and downs, as you do. Life's not simple. Things
don't always work out exactly as you hope they will. I
never saw Ma again. I was angry with her and she was
angry with me. It's my worst regret. Terrible thing,

anger. My little brother told me at her funeral, that she did come to see me once on parade in Whitehall. He said she talked about me all the time after that.

As for Miss West, she wrote to me a few months ago, out of the blue, after she'd seen a picture of me in the paper. She's in a home now, in Sussex, but still hale and hearty at ninety-three. We go and have tea with her, your Grandma and me, and talk about the time when I was Drum Cupboard Monitor. I always feel about ten years old when I'm with her. Funny that. I feel so lucky that we found one another again after so long.

All in all, I've been a lucky lad, luckier than I deserve, that's for sure. I've had my children and my grandchildren, and I've had Grandma with me all these years. It's her that's kept me going. She bucks me up when I need it, and I've needed it a lot, needed her a lot. Sometimes she says I still love Dombey more than I love her, which is not true. But it's a close thing.

Michael Morpurgo

Michael Morpurgo is, in his own words, "oldish, married with three children, and a grandfather six times over." Born in 1943, he attended schools in London, Sussex and Canterbury. He went on to London University to study English and French, followed by a step into the teaching profession and a job in a primary school. It was there that he discovered what he wanted to do:

"We had to read the children a story every day and my lot were bored by the book I was reading. I decided I had to do something and told them the kind of story I used to tell my kids… I could see there was magic in it for them, and realised there was magic in it for me."

In 1976 Michael and his wife, Clare, started the charity 'Farms For City Children' (FFCC), which gives young children from inner city and urban areas an opportunity to work on farms in the heart of the countryside. They now have three farms and Michael is patron to many, many more charities.

Michael divides his time between working with children on the farms and writing. "For me, the greater part of writing is daydreaming, dreaming the dream of my story until it hatches out – the writing down of it I always find hard. But I love finishing it, then… sharing my dream with my readers."

Michael Foreman

Michael Foreman grew up during the Second World War in the fishing village of Pakefield in Suffolk. As the beach was sprinked with mines and covered with barbed wire, bombsites became his playground. His mother ran the Pakefield newsagent and it was during his daily paper round that Michael met a teacher from Lowestoft Art School who encouraged him to attend his Saturday art class for children. Michael's talent was obvious, so his teacher suggested that he come to the art school two afternoons a week, eventually attending the art school full time.

Michael's first book, *The General,* was published while he was still a student at the Royal College of Art in London. Since that first book, Michael has become one of the greatest creators of children's books of recent times. A great traveller, he has illustrated collections of fairytales and legends from all over the world, as well as the works of Dickens, Shakespeare, Roald Dahl, Rudyard Kipling, Robert Louis Stevenson and many others. His most famous, award-winning collaboration is with Michael Morpurgo. This book is their twenty-third book together.

Michael has also written and illustrated an amazing collection of books himself, many based on personal experience, including the autobiographical *War Boy*, which won the Kate Greenaway Medal, and *War Game*, which won the Nestlé Smarties Book Prize.

THE FACTS
BEHIND THE STORY

APPENDIX

YOUNG CRIMINALS IN PRISON :: HOLLESLEY BAY
SUFFOLK PUNCH HORSES :: HORSES IN THE MILITARY

YOUNG CRIMINALS IN PRISON

The introduction of the Borstal system

AT the end of the nineteenth century in England, it was suggested for the first time that boys who committed crimes should be locked up in a separate part of the prison from the older criminals. There they would learn a trade and be encouraged to lead a different kind of life when they were released.

The first such separate wing was in the prison at Borstal, near Rochester. This is why, when many similar wings were set up all over England, boys going to such a place were said to be 'sent to Borstal'.

The boys who were sent had to be twenty-three or younger, and likely to benefit from the strict discipline and hard work involved. They were grouped into 'houses' similar to those in many schools. Each house had a housemaster who would get to know every boy individually so he could encourage them to learn more about the things they liked or were good at. Though this was better than the boys being put in the same part of the prison as the hardened, older inmates, Borstals were still tough places to be sent.

In the 1930s, the British government began to create open Borstals like Hollesley Bay. They didn't have the usual high prison walls. Instead, they allowed the boys to do a variety of jobs on a farm or in a workshop.

The daily routine included a full day's work, regular exercise in a gym and opportunities for continuing their education. After they had been working on the farm or in the workshop for a while, the

Fig. 1:
Boys labouring in a
blacksmiths workshop in
the Borstal on the Isle of
Portland, Dorset, 1945.

Borstal boys were often given their own responsibilities, in order to improve their self-respect and to teach them how to gain the trust and respect of others. When it was judged that a Borstal boy's training had prepared him to lead a better life outside the prison – something that could take between one and three years – he would be released.

Borstals were very strict places though, that often used harsh methods to get the more difficult boys to join in with the prison routine. In 1982 the British Government decided to replace the Borstals with the Young Custody Centres we have today.

HOLLESLEY BAY

The story of an unusual estate

NEAR the coast in Suffolk, Hollesley Bay was originally part of a large private estate. Then, during the Victorian era, it was a college that taught young men about farming before they set off to begin new lives in places like Australia and North America. The college had a stud of Suffolk Punch horses that had been bred on the estate for a long time. (A stud means a group of animals kept for breeding.)

In the late 1930s, the land and the stud were sold to the Prison Commissioners. They opened the Hollesley Bay Borstal in 1938, with six buildings to house the boys on the estate, as well as a gym and an educational building with workshops that taught things like carpentry, welding, shoemaking and farriery (putting shoes on horses), painting, decorating and bricklaying.

In addition to the Suffolk Punch stud, there was also an extensive working farm, including a dairy, a variety of animals such as cows, pigs and chickens, and fields for arable farming. The milk and vegetables produced by the Borstal's farm were used not only in Hollesley Bay Borstal, but were also sent to other prisons in East Anglia and London.

Working on the farm and with the horses in the stud was recognised as an important part of the prisoners' rehabilitation – they were even allowed their own branch of the Young Farmers' Club. During the 1960s, when the numbers of Suffolk Punch horses dwindled drastically, the Prison Service kept up the breed's high profile by numerous appearances at agricultural and 'Horse of the Year' shows.

Fig. 2:
*Maurice Fairhead,
Instructional Officer at
HM Borstal Hollesley
Bay 1946-1970, with
three farriery apprentices.*

FARM HORSES

YOUNG FARMERS' CLUB BOOKLET No. 13

NATIONAL FEDERATION OF YOUNG FARMERS' CLUBS

OAKLINGS :: CANONS CLOSE :: RADLETT :: HERTS

Fig. 3:
*Young Farmers' Club
booklet, issued in 1944.*

In 1983, Hollesley Bay Borstal became a young offenders institution. Then, in 2003, it was decided that there would no longer be a prison farm or a stud. The Suffolk Punch Trust stepped in, launching an appeal to raise money to buy the horses, buildings, land and equipment. They now run the stud and their Heritage, Education and Visitor Centre, which is open to the public, tells the incredible story of Hollesley Bay and gives visitors the chance to meet Suffolk Punch horses.

SUFFOLK PUNCH HORSES

An introduction to an unusual breed

THE Suffolk Punch is one of only three native British heavy horse breeds. (The other two being Shire and Clydesdale.) Heavy breeds are strong and tough, and often referred to as 'cart' or 'draft' horses because they have always been used for heavy farm work.

Although smaller than the Shire or the Clydesdale, the Suffolk Punch, with its short legs and barrel-shaped body, is still very powerful. One of the distinctive things about the breed is the chesnut colouring they all share. Amazingly, every Suffolk Punch alive today is descended from one stallion – Thomas Crisp's Horse of Ufford, foaled in 1768.

Bred to be farm horses, working Suffolk Punches live for a long time and, unlike other heavy breeds, can go for long periods without food. They also don't have feathering (long hair) on their legs and so it is quicker to groom them after muddy field work. Before machines took over the heavy work on most farms, the Suffolk Punch was very popular.

Before machines were widely available, a typical day on the farm began at about 5 a.m. with the head horseman coming to feed the horses. (As Suffolk Punches have small stomachs, they need two hours to digest their food before working, otherwise they can get a severe stomach ache which can be fatal in the worst cases.) Around 6 a.m. the other farm workers would arrive and harness the horses, then at 7 a.m. the field work would begin. Although the men would stop for their lunch, the horses would just stand or have a twenty minute nap before starting work again. (Horses can sleep standing up by locking the joints

Fig. 4:
A Suffolk Punch pairs plough team at work in the field.

Fig. 5:
Head horseman Ted Middleton (third from left), his horsemen and Suffolk Punch horses take a break for lunch.

in their back legs so they don't fall over.) The horses might not have needed food during the day, but they certainly needed lots of water – at least fifteen gallons. (Imagine needing to drink 128 pints of milk!) Then after a hard days work, the horsemen would groom and feed the horses and afterwards turn them out to pasture.

Because of the Suffolk Punch's strength, good temperament, longevity and the fact that they were relatively cheap to feed, they were also popular work horses in towns and cities. During the nineteenth and early twentieth centuries they were often to be found carting coal and hauling heavy goods like barrels of beer for the Truman brewery.

By the early twentieth century, heavy horses like the Suffolk Punch had been replaced by cars and lorries in the cities. They still worked on farms until after the Second World War, when the majority of horses were replaced by tractors. Tractors did not need to be fed and groomed on their day off and could plough much faster than a heavy horse plough team. By the early 1950s, the farm work that had traditionally been done by horses was almost completely done by machines.

Because of this dramatic drop in the demand for heavy horses, populations of the different breeds fell steeply during the twentieth century. The Suffolk Punch breed, which had always had the smallest population, almost became extinct. It was saved by a handful of owners and breeders in the 1960s. Today the Suffolk Punch is on the critical list of the Rare Breeds Survival Trust, with only around 410 pedigree horses registered worldwide.

Fig. 6: A road gang with a horse-powered roller and a team of Suffolk Punch horses.

Fig. 7: A Truman brewery wagon, pulled by a pair of Suffolk Punch horses.

HORSES IN THE MILITARY

Horses in battle and on parade

EVER since people learned to ride, horses were used in warfare to give speed and strength to an army. The cavalry (the soldiers on horseback) were often regarded as an elite fighting force.

The largest recorded number of horses used in battle was during the First World War. Although the trench warfare meant that cavalry charges were not effective – although some did still happen – horses were used widely to transport heavy machinery and supplies across the war-torn terrain. It is estimated that by the end of the First World War, eight million horses had died from both sides.

Many horses in the First World War had previously been used for farming, but nevertheless performed bravely in difficult and frightening situations. A testament to one such horse was printed in a pamphlet issued by the Suffolk Horse Society in the early 1920s. A letter from a junior gunner praised his "beefy chestnut Goliath, which pulled anything and everything without much effort and even replaced entire teams of mules on occasions. When we moved up north to the 'blood bath' he pulled a general supplies wagon (heaped up to break all regulations) alone for days and never turned a hair."

Since the First World War, the majority of horses in the army have been replaced by machines. Now, horses are almost exclusively used for ceremonial duties. For hundreds of years, cavalry regiments marched into battle to the beat of military drums, with the drum horse at the head of the band. Today, drum horses are used by regimental bands on special occasions. Clydesdale are often drum horses, but the army chooses the horse according to its abilities rather than its breed. They employ big, fit horses that are patient and kind, because they have to carry a rider in full dress uniform, plus the ceremonial harness and the 40 kilogram silver kettledrums, and must also stand quietly during their ceremonial duties.

Drum horses start their training when they are about three years old. They are trained for up to two years, until they master the skills needed for ceremonial events. Then they will be ready to take part in events like Trooping the Colour, which marks the Queen's birthday.

Fig. 8: A farrier at work in the field during the First World War.

Fig. 9: A London, Midland and Scottish Railway poster adverstising Trooping the Colour in 1930.

Discover more about Suffolk Punch Horses and the Suffolk Punch Trust at:
www.suffolkpunchtrust.org and www.suffolkhorsesociety.org.uk

ACKNOWLEDGEMENTS

Appendix by Libby Hamilton
with consultant Chris Miller.

PICTURE CREDITS

*Fig. 1, Borstal Blacksmiths © Kurt Hutton/Hulton Archive/Getty Images •
Fig. 2, Maurice Fairhead with three apprentices, reproduced by permission of
his daughter, Mrs Joy Anderson • Fig. 3, Young Farmers' Booklet, issued
1944, photograph © Chris Miller • Fig. 4, Suffolk Punch pairs plough
team, reproduced by permission of the Suffolk Horse Society • Fig. 5, Head
Horseman Ted Middleton and horsemen take a break for lunch, Suffolk Punch horses
owned by Mr Stuart Paul, reproduced by permission of Mr Middleton's daughter
• Fig. 7, Suffolk Punches with Truman's wagon, reproduced by permission
of Mrs Cheryl Grover • Fig. 8, farrier performing field work during the
First World War, reproduced by permission of Mr Ray Hubbard • Fig. 9,
Trooping the Colour LMS Poster (artwork by Christopher Clark),
1930 © National Railway Museum / Science & Society Picture Library*

*While every effort has been made to obtain permissions, the publisher will be
happy to correct any omission in future printings.*